"I'm fascinated with aggressive music on a street level. We draw from all corners of rock 'n' roll history, hip hop, dance, punk, whatever, and spit it out as the Prodigy sound. The live element allows us to take it one step further, to really connect with the crowd and bring out a darker side to the band. It will always remain important to me to create something raw and unpolished."

Liam

poison

"'Poison' introduced lyrics for the first time. It doesn't directly mean anything but people can relate to those words in whichever way they choose. That started to open up other possibilities to the band, both in terms of the gigs and on record."

Maxim

"Performing is the most powerful drug on earth.
I get a come-down if we don't gig for a few weeks, it's unbelievable."

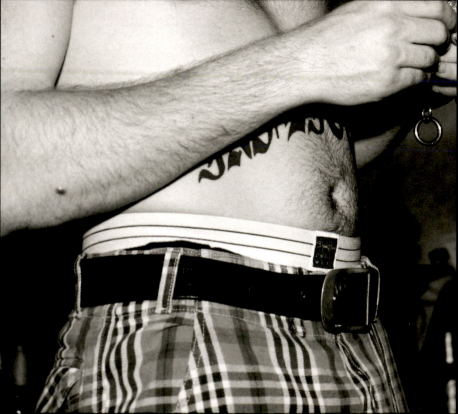

"When the van arrives to pick me up it's great because as soon as we get to the airport I know we are going to have a laugh. As soon as the shows start, we become a unit, one of four people. Within that unit I feel safe."
Maxim

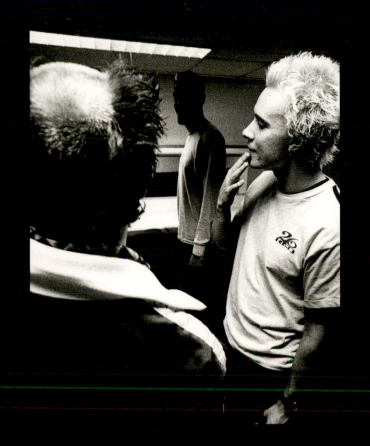

"The first album *Experience* sums up that period of our lives, going to raves, parties, that whole scene. The album is like a show from those times, with all the elements that people were into - piano riffs, rave stuff, all quite anthemic. *Jilted* went much darker, it progressed and took us much further forward. It was more electronic, much less dance-based, introducing more guitar and rock into the band's spectrum. The next album is substantially different again, but constant to all the records is the hardness, that Prodigy edge and sound, that is never absent."

Leeroy

"Before the gig I am not thinking about anything, I keep my mind completely clear and empty. I don't even think of the gig, it's as if I was in a room on my own, I shut all the distractions out and don't like to be bothered by anybody. The first time I start to think of the gig is when we leave the dressing room and head for the stage, but even then I am still empty - it is not until we are introduced that I switch on and rapidly become focussed. I have never had stage fright."

Maxim

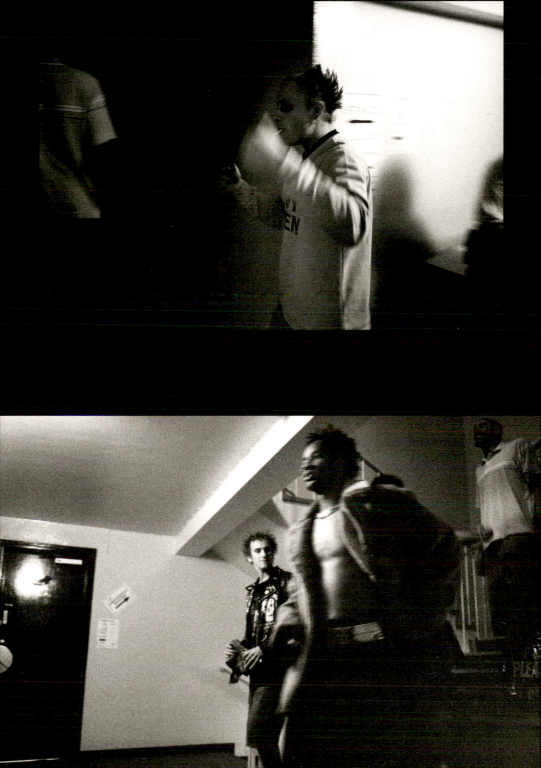

"'Firestarter' was a risk, we had never done a fully vocal track before and Keith had never sung before. It was hardly the safe option. We could have turned out the same old tunes over and over again, but that's not what The Prodigy are about. We are about taking risks."

Maxim

"I spent half the time shouting at people in the crowd anyway, so it was a natural progression from there really, getting it out from my mouth to express myself further. I don't think the lyrics are part of that expression, it's nice if they are truthful to yourself, but that's not what it's all about. The lyrics are just things that sound good, hard and fast, it's more about the noise I make than what I am actually trying to say. The delivery is more important than the message.

You can get very safe going on stage doing the same thing - I had been doing that for five years before 'Firestarter', and I was confident, comfortable. But starting vocals changed that - suddenly I was wondering what would happen. I was telling Liam it was not a problem, easy, but all the time I was shitting myself, but I went out and it went off straight away.

I did a parachute jump just before that first vocals gig and in the plane getting ready to jump was a very similar feeling. The countdown to both was 'My word, what am I doing here?' When those first lyrics came out it was the same as leaping out of the plane. Amazing.

It's not a character, it's me, driven by adrenalin and the amazing music. I enjoy being able to totally express myself, and the band is a good excuse to do that. It's not so much singing as vocal expression."

Keith

"We were in the car listening to the Red Hot Chili Peppers and Keith was saying how he'd love to do some vocals on a tune, and then two weeks later there he was on 'Firestarter'. As soon as I heard the lyrics I knew it was an explanation of himself, totally Keith. It was another element, it seriously enhances the live show."

Leeroy

"When I listen to our old records there are certain elements I still like, I can see why they worked but I would never write like that again. Take 'No Good (Start The Dance)' - it's not a cool sound, it was back then, it was part of that scene, but you need to move on. And I was never happy with the second album *Jilted*. Everyone made a big thing about that record but I was never fully happy. I liked certain songs, maybe six, perhaps, but the rest were not right. The ground-breaking tracks were 'Poison', 'Voodoo', 'Break And Enter' and 'Their Law'. Only four ground-breaking tunes on that album.

   I knew 'Breathe' and 'Firestarter' were good. That created an enormous pressure on me for the next track, but so did my first single 'Charly', so did all the other big tracks along the way. In a strange way I think that's what drives me, at least partly. What drives me even more is that we have the power to put things in the charts that would otherwise not be heard. We have the power to write a piece of music that is fucking hard and anarchic and know that it will get in the charts and fuck up the mainstream."

Liam

"I'd spent years expressing myself with my body and suddenly I had the chance to express myself with my voice."

Keith

"'Firestarter' was like that. Keith heard the track as an instrumental and thought it was wicked and said he couldn't wait to dance to it on stage. He sat there for a while and then said 'I would love to put some vocals on this'. We put the actual vocals down in a London studio, and I can't explain the feeling me and Keith got that night, driving home listening to the tape, playing it over and over again. I knew then it was original, that I had achieved something."

Liam

i'm the trouble starter

punkin' instigator

"All Prodigy music is raw, and that will never change, the production is raw, the sounds are dirty, you can't get away from that. Take it or leave it."

"We'd been away for a year and we needed to come back with a big impact, but just another dance track would not have broken any new ground. As far as I am concerned 'Firestarter' set a whole new level for English music, that's my honest opinion. When people heard that track it was a major turning point. It was so experimental, crossing the barriers between punk and dance. Keith re-invented himself and it was a great introduction to him. It was convincing but not just because it was No.1. The track sounds like it means business, the way Keith delivers the vocals, the music has such attitude. It was a landmark."

Liam

"As far as the rock 'n' roll format in dance music goes, I don't think it's been done before with such full-on attitude. The idea behind that was because no-one else had done it. Everything was right at the time for us to do that."

Liam

"America is exciting to us because they haven't got all the baggage that the UK has. My main concern is the preoccupation with scenes, and the interest in the 'electronic music scene' - what the hell's that? We'll go over there and rock it on our own, we don't need to rely on a scene to survive. We have far more flexibility than other electronic bands as well - some dance bands are too purist and won't go on rock bills, but as far as we're concerned that's too myopic and limiting. We've got no doubts that when things kick off, we can deliver the performance and the music and the goods, that's our side of the bargain."

Liam

"We'll break America, we've been there every year for five years. We'll make it, because we're good and if something's good there are enough cool people in the States to pick up on it. We'll do it and we'll do it the right way...our way."

Leeroy

"What I was yesterday makes me what I am today. And tomorrow...?"

"Backstage Liam's either eating cereal or smoking a joint."

"At the end of the day, if people find me scary, fuck 'em."

"It's important not to get too locked into one way of thinking, some kind of routine or format. That's what happened to me with the first album, *Experience*. I got locked into certain sounds within that rave scene, specific types of songs, and as a result it is quite a one dimensional record. I don't want to do that again."

Liam

"When you first break into the music scene, everyone is so naive. I was only nineteen when it started happening with 'Charly' and I was so into the rave scene - apart from some hip hop, I was blind to everything else."

Liam

"When the music evolved away from the more typically dance-based, keyboard-heavy elements, into what you could call more rock 'n' roll, with guitars and hints of verses and choruses, it opened things up to the band on a totally new level. In many ways, 'Firestarter' represents that turning point, with the full vocal track especially. Having said that, it was hardly traditional, it's not exactly in the conventional pop format, not by a long way. Liam's stuff is still very twisted, even when he dabbles with more accepted forms."

Leeroy

"From day one when I first heard Liam's music I knew the potential was massive - that first tape I heard had a serious impact, it was so original. Every tune he has written since then has been a progression, going off at tangents, doing the opposite of what people expect him to."

Maxim

"Sometimes after only three hours sleep I have a little grizzle but I very rarely bite back."
Keith

"I go in and out of the studio in sporadic periods, I don't go in there for hours on end. I'm looking for that initial vibe, be it from a beat, a sound, a loop, whatever. Nothing is planned, nothing is deliberate."

Liam

i'm the self-inflicted

mind detonator

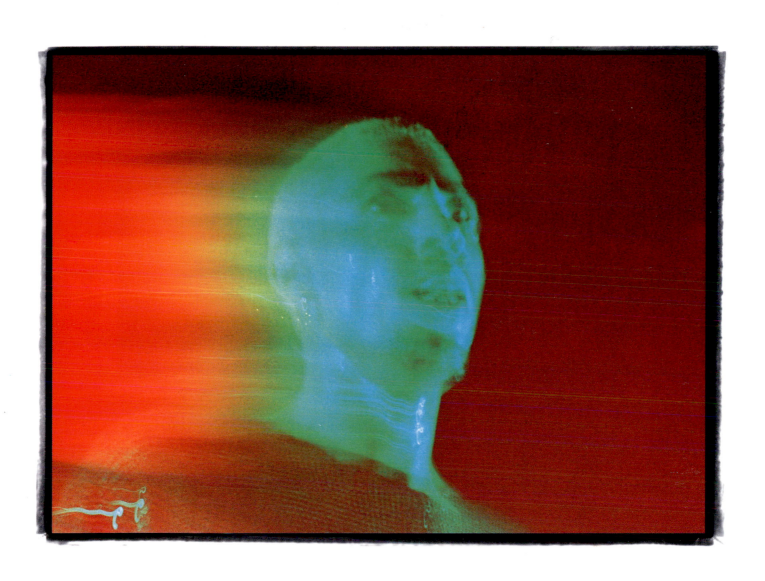

"I get a buzz from being tired during and after a gig. I enjoy that weariness, it tells me I am putting something in. I wouldn't be pleased if I felt fresh at the end of the show. As soon as 'Breathe' kicks in, it all goes mad and I am constantly rolling till the end of the set, which is massively draining."

Maxim

"I enjoy being able to express myself and the band is the perfect way of doing that."
Keith

"Just because someone has green hair doesn't mean they are punk. I have certain attitudes to life and music that don't make me a punk, but in many ways we do have a punk attitude. We set our own rules, so I suppose we are punk in that way."

Maxim

"The firestarter is in him, there's something locked deep and dark inside Keith which drives him forward."

Liam

"Maxim is chilling with old age, like a good wine. He's a cross between me and Keith - when he's on stage he's got that theatrical edge, his commanding stature, people know he's in control of the mike. "

Leeroy

breathe

"The whole idea with the 'Breathe' video was for me and Keith to be confrontational, getting at each other without actually making contact. That concept is very similar to how the track feels on stage - the tension and energy between us is electric. When we play 'Breathe' in the set it just sparks something off. It's a combination of the audience, the sound, the track, it's incredible. We tried to capture that in the video but it's very hard. As with all our videos, I imagined I was performing the song live, you feel it much more that way, but even then it is so hard to recreate that live atmosphere. Performing 'Breathe' live is ten times more powerful and overwhelming."

Maxim

"With 'Breathe' it was completely different to 'Firestarter'. I had already finished the song and they had been dancing to it for several gigs, they knew the song well. Then Keith came up with 'come play my game' in my studio, so we got Maxim round. I rewound the tape and went into another room to sit down. Fifteen minutes later they had the vocals worked out and finished."

Liam

"The music business is like a big trap and that's why I never like to put both feet into it - I like to stand back and laugh at it, because if you jump into the mainstream completely then you are never going to escape.

Songs like 'Firestarter' burst into the mainstream and bend it, twist it. Then we retreat back underground. That's the best way."

Liam

Published in 1997 by INDEPENDENT MUSIC PRESS
This Work is Copyright © Independent Music Press 1997
All Rights Reserved

Exclusive Distributor for the United States and Canada:

OMNIBUS PRESS
A Division of Music Sales
Corporation
257 Park Avenue South
New York, NY 10010 USA

ISBN 1-89-7783-12-4

Designed by Phil Gambrill, Martin Roach and The Prodigy
Interviews by Martin Roach
Photo Credits: Pat Pope: 10, 11, 14-23, 25, 34, 35, 37, 39, 51, 55, 59-61, 70, 72, 78, 82-85, 91, 104, 105; Christian Ammann: 9; Chris Boniface: 89, 93; S. Double/S.I.N: 56; M. Goodacre/S.I.N: 42, 57; Steve Gullick: 3, 28-31, 43, 52, 53, 66, 67; Jamie Harrison: 6, 54, 64, 71; Liam Howlett: 87; Errol Jones: 45, 106-11; Hayley Madden/SIN: 65; Alex Scaglia: 26, 27, 38, 79, 86; Sergey Sergeyev: 1, 8, 33, 44, 62, 69, 76, 81; SIN: 73; Lou Smith: 96, 98, 99, 102, 103; Sharon Thornhill: 4, 5, 12, 13, 46-49, 74, 75, 77, 80, 97, 100, 101; Wright/Wallace: 7, 24, 36, 90, 92, 94, 95
Front and back cover shots: Steve Gullick; Image Manipulation by Tony Campbell
'Poison' photography by Jonathan Rose; 'Breathe' photography by Mary Farbrother;
Every effort has been made to correctly acknowledge and credit the photographers herein. However, should any error or omission appear, it is unintentional, and the publisher should be contacted immediately.

Copyright Notices: 'Firestarter' Words & Music by Liam Howlett, Keith Flint, Trevor Horn, Anne Dudley, Jon Jeczalik, Paul Morley, Gary Langan and Kim Deal © 1995, Reproduced by permission of EMI Virgin Music Ltd, London WC2H 0EA

Printed in Milan, Italy.

 Independent Music Press
P.O.Box 14691
London
SE1 3ZJ

internet: http://www.rise.co.uk/imp
e-mail: imp@ftech.co.uk
fax: 0171 357 8608